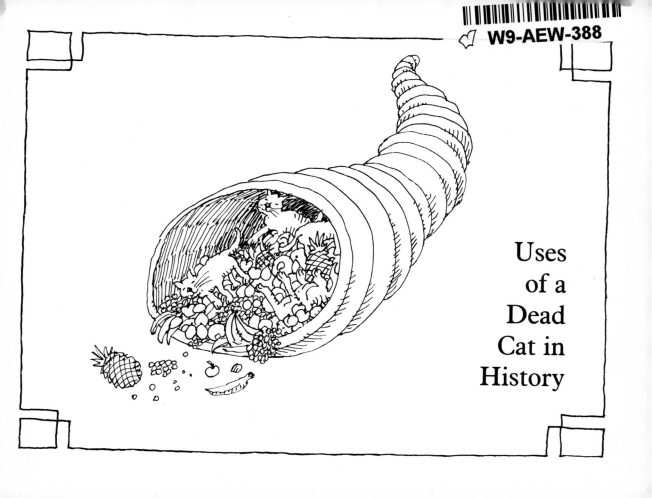

Uses
of a
Dead
Cat in
History

SIMON BOND

Uses of a Dead Cat in History

Mandarin

USES OF A DEAD CAT IN HISTORY

First published in paperback in Great Britain in 1992
by Mandarin Paperbacks, Michelin House, 81 Fulham Road, London SW3 6RB

Mandarin is an imprint of the Octopus Publishing Group,
a division of Reed International Books Ltd

Copyright © 1992 Simon Bond
The author has asserted his moral rights

A CIP catalogue record for this book is available from the British Library
ISBN 0 7493 1212 2

Printed in Great Britain by
St Edmundsbury Press Ltd, Bury St Edmunds, Suffolk

THE ORIGINAL CAST

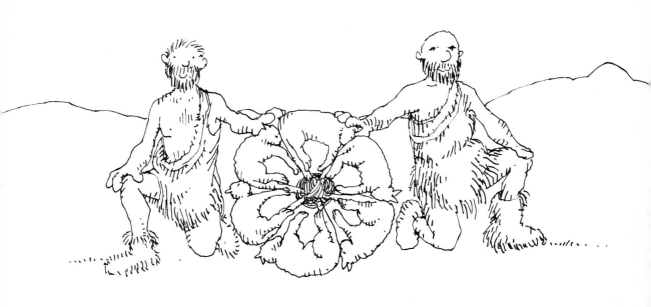

NERG AND OOMA INVENT THE WHEEL

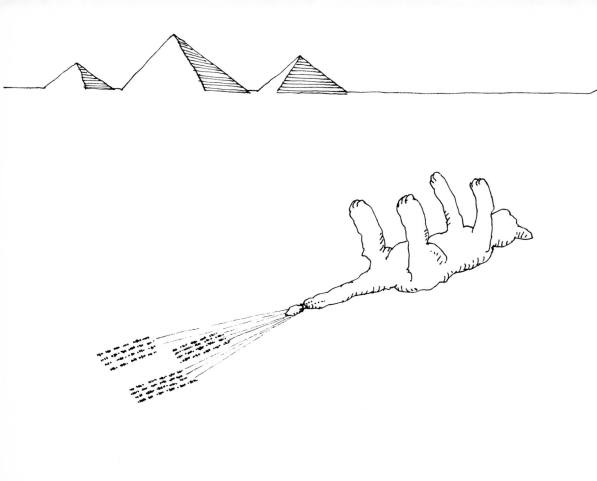

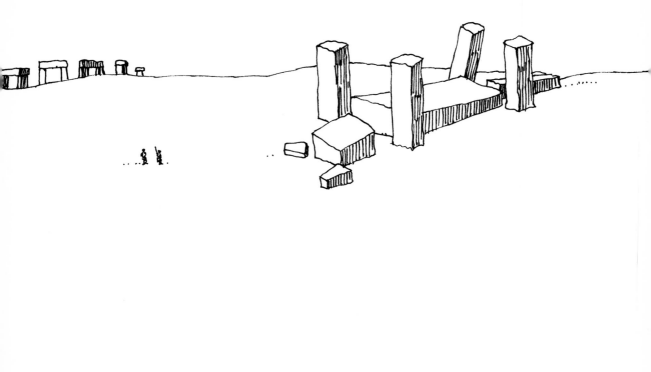

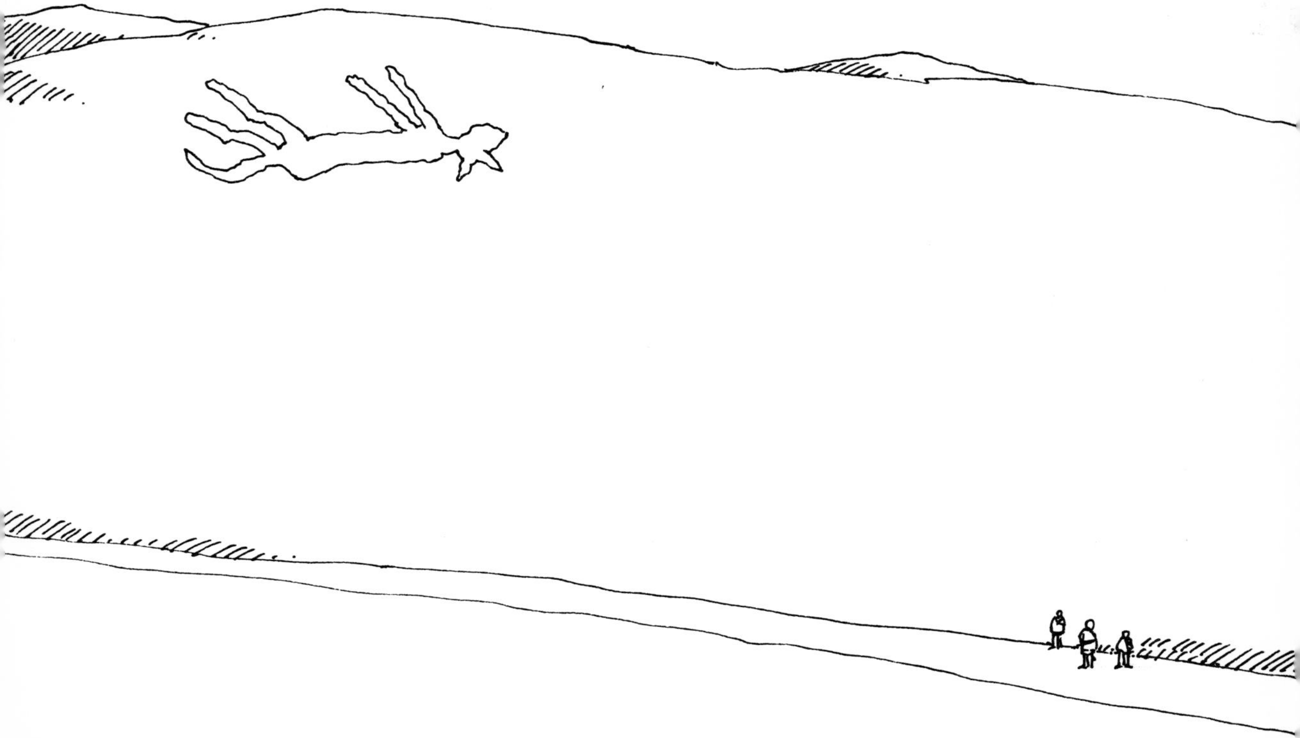

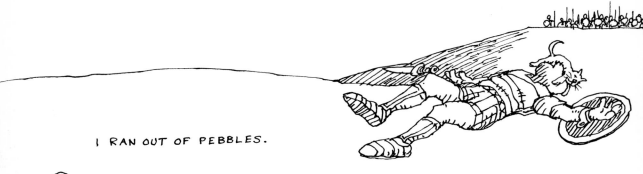

I RAN OUT OF PEBBLES.

AND AFTER THE PLAGUE OF LOCUSTS...

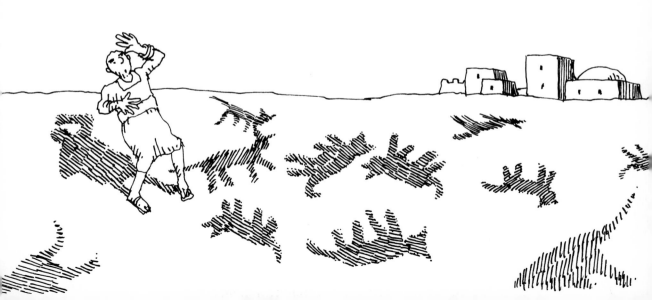

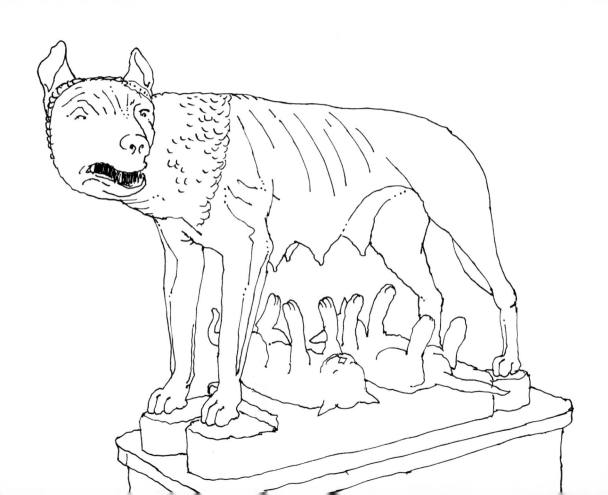

ET TU FLUFFY? **44** BC

'I think you'd better do the fish again.'

1493

CHRISTOPHER COLUMBUS DISCOVERS
A USE FOR THE POTATO

'They don't roll very well, Sir Francis.'

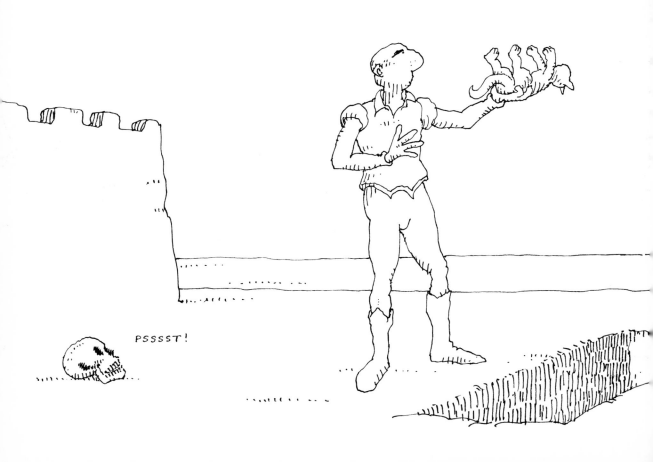

PSSSST!

'Er . . . do you have anything else?'

1667

ISAAC NEWTON IS REMINDED ABOUT GRAVITY

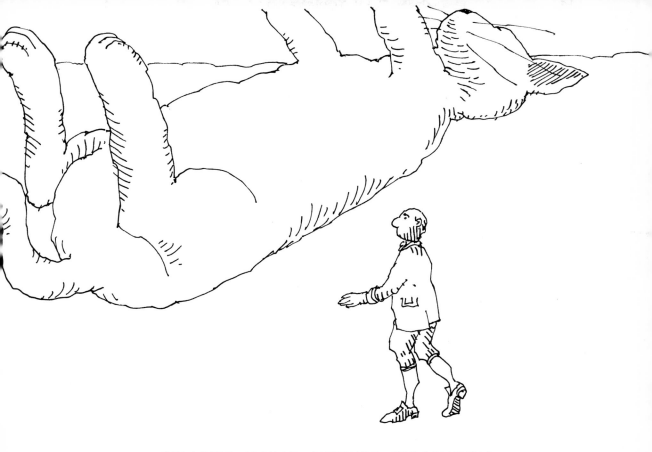

GULLIVER MAKES ANOTHER DISCOVERY

...BECAUSE IT'S QUIET
AND DOESN'T EAT MUCH.

1752

'It's got a message, Master . . . but I don't think we should touch it.'

MONSTROSITIES of 1821

G. Cruikshank

Pub.d by G. Humphrey 27 St James St London May 30 1821

OLIVER DOES NOT ASK FOR MORE

. . .AND PROBABLY WITH A
REASONABLY BLUNT INSTRUMENT.

MAFEKING — STILL WAITING TO BE RELIEVED

MOSCOW 1917

THE MARX BROTHERS
GROUCHO, HARPO, CHICO & STIFFO

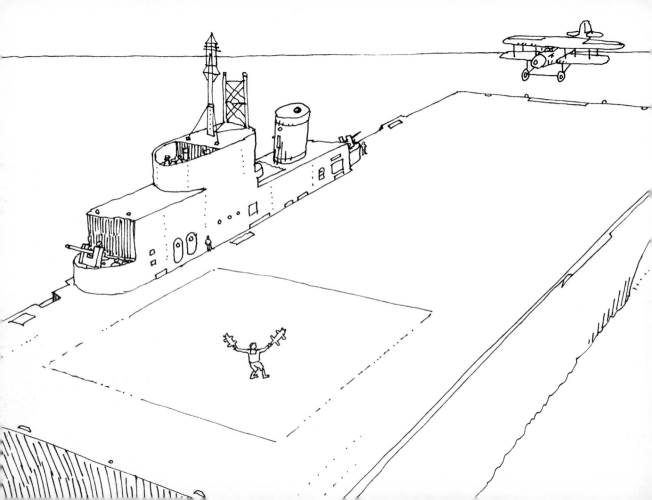

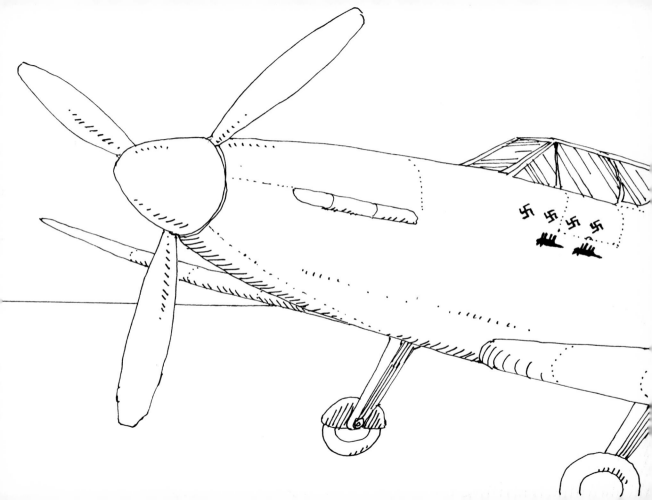

DIMBO

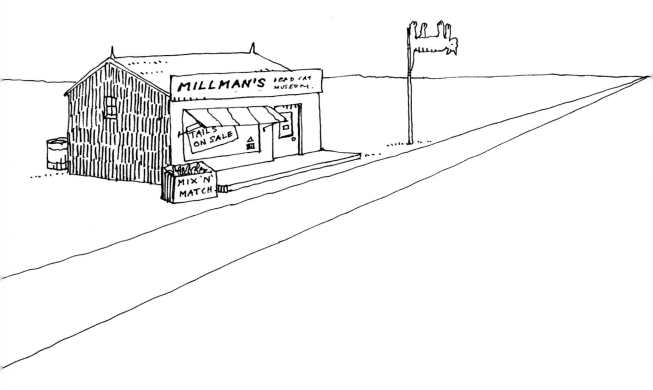

MILLMAN'S DEAD CAT MUSEUM & CURIO SHOPPE (WOOLALOONA FLATS. N.S.W. AUSTRALIA)

FELIX MORT LODGE
TITUSVILLE, NEBRASKA, 1952

1957

SPUTNIK

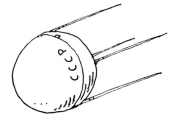

CATNIK

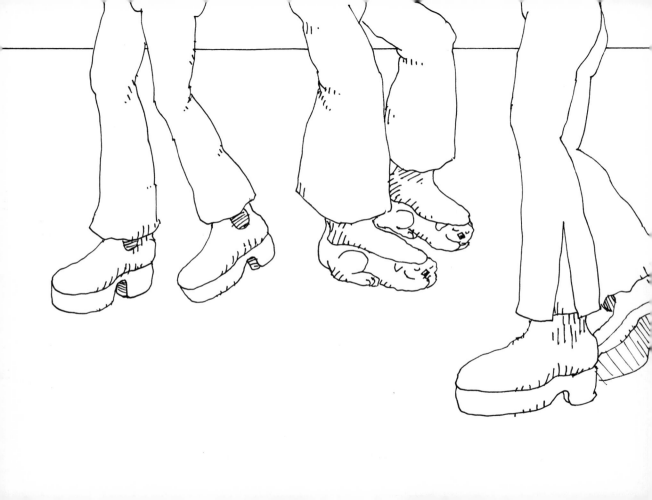

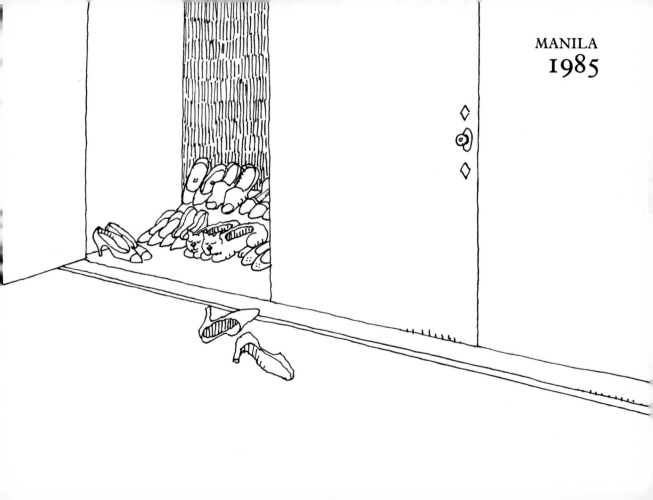

MANILA
1985

BERLIN
1989

WHERE'S THE
BATHROOM?

HEY. THESE ARE MY
KIND OF PEOPLE...

I DON'T GET IT.